The usage of th  g......ure

Gholamreza Asadollahfardi
Rashin Asadollahfardi

The usage of the polluted water for agriculture

Wastewater reuse , Health aspect, Guidelines and standards, Methods of treatment for irrigation

LAP LAMBERT Academic Publishing

Impressum/Imprint (nur für Deutschland/only for Germany)
Bibliografische Information der Deutschen Nationalbibliothek: Die Deutsche
Nationalbibliothek verzeichnet diese Publikation in der Deutschen Nationalbibliografie;
detaillierte bibliografische Daten sind im Internet über http://dnb.d-nb.de abrufbar.
Alle in diesem Buch genannten Marken und Produktnamen unterliegen warenzeichen-,
marken- oder patentrechtlichem Schutz bzw. sind Warenzeichen oder eingetragene
Warenzeichen der jeweiligen Inhaber. Die Wiedergabe von Marken, Produktnamen,
Gebrauchsnamen, Handelsnamen, Warenbezeichnungen u.s.w. in diesem Werk berechtigt
auch ohne besondere Kennzeichnung nicht zu der Annahme, dass solche Namen im Sinne
der Warenzeichen- und Markenschutzgesetzgebung als frei zu betrachten wären und
daher von jedermann benutzt werden dürften.

Coverbild: www.ingimage.com

Verlag: LAP LAMBERT Academic Publishing GmbH & Co. KG
Dudweiler Landstr. 99, 66123 Saarbrücken, Deutschland
Telefon +49 681 3720-310, Telefax +49 681 3720-3109
Email: info@lap-publishing.com

Approved by: This is my work at my university as a faculty member

Herstellung in Deutschland:
Schaltungsdienst Lange o.H.G., Berlin
Books on Demand GmbH, Norderstedt
Reha GmbH, Saarbrücken
Amazon Distribution GmbH, Leipzig
ISBN: 978-3-8465-1196-1

Imprint (only for USA, GB)
Bibliographic information published by the Deutsche Nationalbibliothek: The Deutsche
Nationalbibliothek lists this publication in the Deutsche Nationalbibliografie; detailed
bibliographic data are available in the Internet at http://dnb.d-nb.de.
Any brand names and product names mentioned in this book are subject to trademark,
brand or patent protection and are trademarks or registered trademarks of their respective
holders. The use of brand names, product names, common names, trade names, product
descriptions etc. even without a particular marking in this works is in no way to be
construed to mean that such names may be regarded as unrestricted in respect of
trademark and brand protection legislation and could thus be used by anyone.

Cover image: www.ingimage.com

Publisher: LAP LAMBERT Academic Publishing GmbH & Co. KG
Dudweiler Landstr. 99, 66123 Saarbrücken, Germany
Phone +49 681 3720-310, Fax +49 681 3720-3109
Email: info@lap-publishing.com

Printed in the U.S.A.
Printed in the U.K. by (see last page)
ISBN: 978-3-8465-1196-1

Table of Contents

1. Introduction

A rapidly increasing population coupled with increased urbanization and its associated high water consumption has forced people to use wastewater for agricultural and in some cases for drinking purposes. This phenomenon is not new.

The application of wastewater for irrigation purposes was adopted in Germany and England when sewage farms were first developed in the nineteenth century. In the United States of America the need for irrigation water has led to the use of sewage effluent for the primary purpose of crop production at early stages. California whose agriculture is heavily dependent on irrigation is still one of the leaders in the field of effluent reuse. The California State Board of Health in 1918 passed regulations prohibiting the use of raw sewage for irrigation of most garden crops to be eaten raw. Crops that were to be eaten cooked could be irrigated, but only if done so at least 30 days before harvesting.

Fruits, nut trees and melons which did not come in contact with sewage, were excluded from the 1918 regulations. These regulations were modified in 1933. With the passage of the Dickey Water Pollution Act in 1949, it became necessary to gain permission from the California State Regional Water Pollution Control Board to use reclaimed wastewater. Further revisions were made in 1969 and 1978 (Aikman, 1983).

In many other areas of the world, particularly Africa and the Middle East, irrigation with sewage polluted waters have been carried out on an informal basis for a number of years, sometimes with serious health hazards. Over the last three decades, British consultants have been heavily involved in the design of joint effluent treatment and irrigation schemes in the area (Aikman, 1983).

The use of effluents to irrigate parks, lawns, central reservations on highways and other open public areas is widespread, especially in the Middle East. Tanks sometimes bring effluents from the treatment works to the city center. This type of irrigation is only acceptable using the effluents from waste stabilization ponds or tertiary treatment processes and, even then, very careful monitoring of their pathogen content is required. Compared to other reuse techniques the irrigation of amenity areas is a high-risk activity.

Yang and Abbaspour (2007) analyzed wastewater reuse possible under various driving forces and constraint of Beijing in China. They applied a linear programming model to analyze different reuse scenarios concerning alternative wastewater charges and reuse costs. Their consequences propose that the wastewater reuse potential is elevated at competitive prices. Wastewater treatment plants come into view to be more economically efficient over on-site operation facilities in providing treated wastewater for reuse

Carr et al. (2010) applied a multi-disciplinary study method to illustrate that soil reaction to irrigation with reclaimed water is a function of the management strategies accepted on the farm by

1

the water consumer. The acceptance of management techniques to keep soil productivity can be seen to be a consequence of farmers' awareness of potentially plant-toxic ions in the irrigation water (70% of Jordan Valley cultivator recognized the salinity as a risk from irrigation with wastewater reuses). Organizational interviews make known that institutional awareness of soil management challenges was fairly elevated (34% of interviewees explained salinity as a risk from water reuse); however, the strategies to lecture to this challenge at the institutional level need superior progress.

Alfarra et al. (2011) revealed that no single source could fully solve water shortage in Jourdan. They suggested the treated wastewater for irrigation purposes in Jordan.

Alfarra et al. (2011) stated that the treated wastewater will have the major potential to supplement water supply in the near future, so narrowing the gap between available freshwater and total demand. Treated wastewater might be a valuable source for irrigation in the agricultural division and a rising percentage of irrigated areas.

Raniern et al (2011) studied the using treated wastewater for food crop irrigation in Adelaide, South Australia; Foggia, South Italy and Monterey, California. A comparison between them showed that the dissimilarity in the complexity of the technological treatments were because of different regulations; therefore, first they recommended a standardization of the regulation for around the world where standards should be tackled more to microbial community and pathogenic than to chemical elements. Second, it was also strongly proposed the improvement of wastewater reuse for the world since the impact of climate change on water resources. Third, it was suggested the improvement of the artificial ground water recharge since this is very significant in groundwater management and mainly where the conjunctive use of surface water and groundwater resources are considered. Finally regarding the salinity, this limit should be according to the characteristic of the crops and of the source water.

Due to the shortage of water in Iran, raw-wastewater diluted with surface water is illegally used. Considering the dangers, the government attempted to produce regulations on the use of these waters for agricultural purposes. The faculty of public health and hygiene at Tehran University, has investigated the use of polluted water of a stream for agricultural purpose (Ehrampush, 1988). Also Bagargan in 1988 investigated the effects of heavy metals present in a stream on the soil, and the produced vegetation.

The first aim of this book is to review the existing literature about waste water reuse for agricultural purposes , and second is to study of the existing situation of the surface water quality for applying for crop cultivation.

In this book we describe health aspects, Consumers Plants, Quality requirements for irrigation with sewage water, Effect of chemical pollutant , methods of water quality improvement for agricultural purposes and conclusion.

2.   Health Aspects

There is some element of risk in public exposure in almost every reclamation operation, but in general, the health concern is proportional to the degree of human contact with the water and the adequacy and reliability of the treatment process. Where exposure is unlikely, the health risk is limited, but it increases when direct or indirect exposure is probable.

The public should be well informed on matters concerning advantages and possible health hazards arising from the agricultural reuse of municipal wastewater. The health hazards are of four kinds:

1- Agricultural field workers and their families;

2-Crop-handlers;

3-Consumers (of crops, meat and milk); and

4-Those living near the affected fields (EPA, 1992).

The only way to protect farmers is to use the wastes that are pathogen-free or nearly so. A special problem regarding health occurs when spray irrigation of sewage effluent is used.

Bacteria and viruses in aerosols remain viable and travel farther with increased wind velocity, increased relative humidity, lower temperature and darkness (Hicky and Reist, 1975). Vegetable decontamination studies have indicated that washing vegetables with water or detergents is ineffective in removing bacteria and helminth eggs. Helminth eggs are also extremely resistant to chemical disinfectants (Crook, 1978).

A recent study of several farms in Israel which use undisinfected wastewater for crop irrigation indicated that the incidence of shigellosis, salmonellosis, infectious hepatitis and typhoid fever were substantially higher than in populations of similar agricultural area that did not use wastewater for irrigation (Katzenelson et al, 1976).

In India untreated sewage is extensively used for irrigation with little personal hygiene practiced by workers. The result is that hookworm and other enteric infections are very common. On the other hand, in the USA and Australia, where treated wastewater is used and reasonable personal hygiene is adopted no such occurrences have been recorded (Ali, 1987). The risks from contaminated products depend very largely on the type of product or the use to which it is put. These are described in the following sections.

Shuval et al. (1997) studied the annual risk of infectious hepatitis from regularly eating vegetables irrigated with raw wastewater. Their results were shown it was as elevated as 10^{-3}. The study pointed out that the annual risk of succumbing to a virus illness from frequently eating vegetables irrigated with effluent meeting WHO guideline is insignificant and is 10^{-6} to 10^{-7}.

3

Srikanth and Naik (2004) investigated about the effect of the use of the raw domestic sewage for vegetable farming in the suburbs of the capital of Asmara, Eritra. The consequence indicated heavy contamination of vegetables by faecal coli forms in addition to with Giardia cysts. By the investigation they found both faecal coli forms and Giardia cysts exist in the stool of the some people live in the area and eat raw vegetable such as lettuce and cabbage.

El Ayni et al (2011) assessed the environmental and health impact that would have the reuse of treated wastewater for harvests direct irrigation or for the recharge of the local aquifer in Korba (Tunisia).They analyzed the treated wastewater for recharging of the aquifer. There was no pollution by organic matter or heavy metals were revealed; however, elevated salinity, nitrate, potassium and chloride concentrations were noticed. The monitored data showed bacteriological incidence of faecal streptococcus, crop thermo-tolerant coliforms, total coliforms and E coli, but absence of salmonella.

The consequence of season and wastewater storage on the risk of Ascaris Zumbricoides infection and diarrhoeal illness connectd with wastewater reuse was envestigated in Mexico in 199 1. Data were gathered from 10 489 persons during a dry-season survey. Exposure was to untreated wastewater, or effluent from 1 reservoir (c 1 nematode egg/L), or no wastewater irrigation (control group). The consequences were contrastd with a preceding wet-season study which containd effluent from 2 reservoirs in series. Direct contact to untreated wastewater was associated with an surplus risk of A. Zumbricoides infection in kids aged < 5 years (OR = 18.0) and people aged > 5 years (OR = 13.5) and an boost risk of diarrhoea,mainly to kids aged < 5 years (OR = 1.75); the results were more powerful in the dry than in the wet season.There was also an surplus risk associated with the 1-reservoir group for A. lumbricoides infection (OR = 2 1.2 and 9.4) and for diarrhoeal illness (OR = 1.1 and 1.5) ;however, little excess associated with the 2-reservoir sgroup. consequently, wastewater retention in 1 reservoir (quality lo5 faecal coliforms/lOO mL, c 1 egg/L)does not significantly reduce risks of Ascarzs infection and diarrhoeal disease whereas retention in 2reservoirs in series (quality 1 O3 faecal coliforms/ 100 mL, no detectable eggs/L) does(Ursula et al. ,2001).

3. Consumers of plants

As a man or animal consumes agricultural products, their lives can be considered as hazardous. There are two types of effects.

1) Effects of biological pollutant; and

2) Effects of chemical pollutant.

3.1 Effect of biological pollutant

The main point of concern here is the health risk to those who handle, prepare or eat the crop after it has been harvested. All types of pathogens in the untreated effluent may reach the field unless effectively removed by a reliable treatment process. If they reach into the field, can be hazardous depending on their concentration, survival times, possibility of being translocated to the crop and hence to man. Survival times on the soil can be generalized for various pathogens. This is illustrated in Table 1.

Pathogen	Survival time
Viruses	Up to six months; Generally less than three months.
Bacteria	Over a year; Generally less than two months.
Protozoa	Up to ten days; Generally less than two days.
Helminth	Up to seven years; Generally less than two years.

Table 1 Survival times of various pathogens in soil (Aikman, 1983)

The method of irrigation and the type of crop determine the possibility of pathogen being attached to the surface of the crop. Waste's application may be discontinued one month before harvesting in the hope that all pathogens will die before the harvest. Once on the crop, pathogen survival is not very long compared to survival in soil. The survival time for various types of excreted pathogens on crop surfaces is shown in Table 2.

Pathogen	Survival time
Viruses	Up to two months; Generally less than one month.
Bacteria	Up to six months, Generally less than one month.
Protozoa	Up to five days; Generally less than two days.
Helminths	Up to five months; Generally less than one month.

Table 2 The survival times of various excreted pathogens on crop surfaces (Aikman, 1983)

Pathogen	Fresh Water & Sewage	Crops	Soil
Viruses [a]			
Enteroviruses [b]	< 120 but usually <50	< 60 but usually <15	< 100 but usually <20
Bacteria			
Faecal coliforms [a]	< 60 but usually <30	< 30 but usually <15	< 70 but usually <20
Salmonella spp [a]	< 60 but usually <30	< 30 but usually <15	< 70 but usually <20
Shigella spp [a]	< 30 but usually <10	< 10 but usually <5	
Vibrio cholerae [c]	< 30 but usually <10	< 5 but usually <2	< 20 but usually <10
Protozoa			
Entamoeba Histolytica cysts	< 30 but usually <15	< 10 but usually <2	< 20 but usually <10
Helminths			
Ascaris Lumbricoides eggs	Many months	< 60 but usually <30	Many months
a) In seawater, viral survival is less, and bacterial survival is very much less than in fresh water.			
b) Includes polio-, echo-, and coxsackieviruses.			
c) Cholerae survival in aqueous environments is a subject of current uncertainty.			

Table2A   Typical Pathogen Survival Times (days) at 20-30 ° C   (EPA, 1992)

The most lethal factors in killing off pathogens are dryness and direct sunshine. Survival may be expected to be much lower in dry, sunny climates than under humid and damp conditions. Table 2A shown the survival time for some types of excreted pathogen crop surfaces and soils at temperature between 20-30 degree centigrade. Survivals are quite sufficient, however, for viable pathogens to be transported into markets, factories, and homes and subsequently infect those who handle process, prepare or eat the crop.

Beef-tapeworm and some other animal pathogens are encountered in sewage from time to time. The helminth circulates between man and cattle and infection only occurs when cattle eat these eggs, especially Taenia eggs that are excreted from humans. Therefore, any reuse that brings cattle into direct contact with human excreta may promote the transmission of the disease, unless adequate treatment is provided. Taenia ova are quite resistant and may survive in soil or on pasture for over six months (Aikman, 1983).

Bacteria and viruses in wastewater present a major health hazard in agricultural reuse. Water borne diseases include amoebic dysentery and bacillary, cholera, briosis, salmonellosis, leptospirosis and infectious hepatitis. Some other diseases, which are less common, are ascariasis, schistosomiasis, brucellosis, ancylostomia and tapeworm. Epidemiological evidence from other countries shows that several disease outbreaks have occurred in the past due to the consumption of irrigation with sewage (Crook, 1978).

The effluent used for unrestricted agricultural reuse is of a very high bacteriological and virological quality. Therefore foods crop for raw consumption or when brought raw into the kitchen, can be included in the effluent irrigation scheme without any health hazard.

A high bacteriological quality is also important in order to minimize the danger of aerosols spreading organisms during sprinkler irrigation and improving the public acceptance of the effluent.

3.2 Effect of chemical pollutant

Many of the chemical determinands are not toxic to plants themselves but are harmful to consumers. Nitrate is one of examples of chemical pollutants and plants like pigweed take up as much as 10,000 to 15,000 ppm (Uriu, 1971). Accumulation of nitrate in forage crops such as Sudan grain and corn may cause health problems and can cause problems in two ways:

1) Nitrogen oxide gases that are deadly to animals and;

2) A high concentration of nitrate causes injuries when consumed by animals (Crawford and Kennedy, 1960). The nitrate is converted to nitrite in the blood to form the non-oxygen transporting metheomoglobin resulting in cyanides.

Most heavy metals are precipitated in the sewage sludge of secondary sewage treatment and are thus kept out of the effluent to be used for irrigation. However, soluble heavy metal chelates are formed from the combination of heavy metals and organic in the sewage effluent. The harmful effects on plants of heavy metals, such as arsenic, lead, and copper, are the biggest unknowns in the use of sewage effluent for irrigation (Baier and Fryer, 1973).

Once heavy metals have reached toxic levels in the soil solution, they are difficult to remove. Many heavy metals are not removed by leaching because of their affinity with the soil, while tillage practices simply redistribute the heavy metals throughout the plough layer of the soil (Baier and Fryer, 1973).

Lead is another chemical determinand whose excess is harmful to plant consumer. For example lead applied to forage foliage in an aerosol is toxic to horses when the concentration in the forage is between 4 to 100 ppm (Rains, 1971).

Cow or sheep with pH of 6.5 to 7.0 in their digestive tract, precipitate the lead in their rumens. Soluble lead can cause total brain damage (Baier and Fryer, 1973).

Another chemical determinand, which is harmful to the plant consumer, is Molybdenum. Alfalfa, clover grasses can be toxic to plant consumer if the level of Molybdenum in the plant reaches 15 ppm to 20 ppm.

In comparison with the health problems associated with biological contaminants, the health problem associated with chemical contaminants are less significant. Some diseases relative to chemical contaminant is shown in Table 3 (Cowan and Johnson, 1984).

Chemical contaminant	Disease
Lead	Lead Poisoning
Nitrate	Methaemoglobinaemia
Sodium	Hypernatratmia
Organic halogens	Cancer
Poly nuclear aromatic hydrocarbons	Cancer

Table 3 Contaminants in wastewater and associated diseases

4.   Quality requirements for irrigation with sewage water

Irrigation is an excellent use of sewage effluent because it is mostly water with nutrients. There are, however, other substances in the effluent that could adversely affect the crop, the soil, the underlying groundwater, the farm workers, and/or the consumers (human and animal) of the crops.

In order to determine the suitability of a given effluent for irrigation or the quality requirements for irrigation of certain crop, the chemical and biological composition of the effluent should be known and its effect evaluated.

Bixio et al. (2006) believed that" It is necessary to have clearer institutional arrangements, economic instruments and water reuse guidelines for wastewater reuse implementation; however, technological innovation and the establishment of a best practice framework can be few more urgent and critical goals than to create an alter in the underlying stakeholders' perception."

Blumenthal et al. (2000) reviewed the three dissimilar moves towards for establishing guidelines for the microbiological quality of treated wastewater .The approaches had different purposes as their results: : the absence of fecal indicator organisms in the wastewater, the absence of a quantifiable excess of cases of enteric illness in the exposed population and a model-generated estimated risk underneath a defined acceptable risk. If the second approach (using empirical epidemiological studies supplemented by microbiological studies of the transmission of pathogens) is employed in conjunction with the third approach (using a model-based quantitative risk assessment for selected pathogens) an influential tool is created that assists the development of regulations. The first approach is less cost effective than the combined method and less sufficiently protect public health. The guideline limit for for faecal coliform bacteria in unrestricted irrigation <1000 faecal coliform bacteria/100 ml is official, however for restricted irrigation <10^5 faecal coliform bacteria/100 ml is suggested while adult farm workers are exposed to spray irrigation. A limit of<10^3 faecal coliform bacteria/100 ml is proposed if flood irrigation is employed or children are exposed. The guideline boundary for nematode eggs for both types of irrigation is sufficient except when conditions good turn the survival of nematode eggs and wherever children are exposed; in these cases it should be decreased from <1 egg/l to <0.1 egg/l (Blumenthal, 2000).

Jimenez (2005) studied the waste reuse of the Tula Valley case in Mexico as a case study. It was ended that with a suitable regulation and wastewater treatment technology a win–win move toward to safely reuse wastewater in agriculture at a reasonable cost may be possible.

4.1 Salinity

Soil-water salinity is commonly expressed as the electrical conductivity (COND) of the saturation extracts of the soil and is a common water quality factor affecting the plant growth. The maximum permissible salt concentration of irrigation water is governed by the salt tolerance of the crop. Crops tend to be more sensitive to salt in irrigation water at the early stages of growth than later in the growing season. There are also limits on the allowable total salt content of irrigation water because leaching requirements may become impractical, requiring very frequent large irrigation. Even then, crop yields may be reduced because the average salt concentration in the root zone may become too high. In view of these considerations, it is difficult to prescribe maximum salt concentration for irrigation water. The classification prepared by Ayres is shown is Table 4.

Electrical conductivity (COND) ds/m (mmho/cm)	Degree of problem
COND <0.75	No problem
0.75< COND <3	Slight to moderate
COND >3	Severe

Table 4   The degree of problem according to the conductivity value

Sewage effluents will typically have a salt concentration of 0.45-3 ds/m (mmho/cm) and mostly will lie in the range of 0.6 to 1.2 ds/m (mmho/cm).

4.2 Sodium and permeability hazard

The degree to which sodium will be absorbed by a soil is a function of the proportion of sodium to the divalent cautions (Ca and Mg), and is usually expressed by the sodium adsorbtion ratio (SAR) given as:

$$SAR = \frac{Na}{\sqrt{\dfrac{Ca^{++} + Mg^{++}}{2}}}$$

The hydraulic conductivity of the soil is also affected by the salt concentration of the soil solution. The higher the salt concentration of the soil solution, the higher the soil hydraulic conductivity will be for a given SAR. Sodium also has adverse effects on the crops, such as leaf burn.

Ayers and Tanji (1981) have expressed the degree of the problem according to the level of SAR_{adj} as it is illustrated in Table 5. SAR_{adj} can be estimated by:

$$SAR_{adj} = SAR[\ 9.4 - p(k_2 - k_c) - p(Ca + Mg) - P(ALK)]$$

PK_2 = Negative logarithm of the second dissociation constant for carbonic acid,

10

PK_c = Solubility Constant for Calcite,

P = Negative logarithm of ion concentrations (meg/L).

SAR_{adj}	Level of Problem
Less than 3	No Problem
Between 3 and 4	Increasing-Problems
Greater than 9	Severe Problems

Table 5 The degree of problems according to the SARadj level

If the leaves absorb the water, as with the sprinkler irrigation, there are no problems if the sodium concentration of the irrigation water is below 70 meg/L. However, the problems will increase as it gets above 70 meq/L (Ayers and Tanji, 1981).

4.3 Nitrogen

This constituent of wastewater is of many forms and has a fertilizing effect in irrigated agriculture. However, an excess of nitrogen has an adverse effect. With each mg/l of nitrogen contained, in wastewater, about 2.7 lb./acre N is applied with each foot of irrigation water. Table 6 shows the amounts of nitrogen applied by irrigation with sewage effluent with N concentrations of 5-50 mg/l and at water application ratios of 1-5 ft (0.3-1.5m). Considering that the nitrogen concentration in raw wastewater or secondary effluent are generally within the range of 15-40 mg/l, and that the normal irrigation water application in dry, warm areas is 3-6 ft/year, the nitrogen application with effluent would normally vary about 120-650 lb/acre per year. These higher values are in excess the amounts of nitrogen required by crops.

Another problem related to the use of nitrogen in effluent as fertilizer is that the water demand and the nitrogen demand are not in parallel. For most crops, nitrogen demands is highest during the period of active growth and lowest during the initial growth stages and when harvests time approaches.

Nitrogen concentration in effluent (mg/l)	Water Application (ft/yr)				
	1 (2)	2 (3)	3 (4)	4 (5)	5 (6)
05	14	28	42	56	70
10	27	54	81	108	135
15	41	81	122	162	203
20	54	108	162	216	270
25	68	135	203	270	338
30	81	162	243	324	405
35	95	189	284	378	473
40	108	216	324	432	540
45	122	243	365	486	608
50	1135	270	405	540	675

Note:

1 Ib/acre = 1.12 kg/ha.

Table 6 Nitrogen application (1b/acre) by irrigation with effluent (Bouwer and Idelovitch, 1987)

Where nitrogen applications exceed crop nitrogen requirements, higher nitrogen concentrations in the deep percolating water can be expected. Thus sewage irrigation should be carefully managed, and nitrate in underlying groundwater should be monitored to make sure that undesirable nitrate pollution of the groundwater does not occur. Suggested nitrate contents from WHO and European standards are illustrated in Tables 7 and 8.

	Suggested Nitrate Contents	
	As NO_3	As N
Maximum Desirable	45	10.2
Maximum Permissible	--	--

Table 7 Suggested nitrate content *WHO*

	Suggested Nitrate Contents	
	As NO$_3$	As N
Maximum Desirable	50	11.3
Maximum Permissible	100	22.6

Table 8   European Standard (Burfield, 1977)

4.4 Phosphorus

This is another major nutrient found in wastewater, which has, in general, a beneficial effect on crops. The rate of uptake by some crops is shown in Table 9

Crop	Alfalfa	Bromegrass	Coastal Bermuda Grass	Kentucky Bluegrass	Barley	Corn	Cotton	Potatoes	Soybeans	Wheat
Up take (lb/acre year)	20-30	35-50	30-40	40	15	17-25	12	14	11-18	15

Table 9   The rate of nutrient uptake for some crops (Bouwer and Idelovitch, 1987)

However, phosphorus excess may have a negative effect on crops and soils. It can cause crop to yield reduction due to the nutrient imbalance. The normal phosphorus concentration is about 5-10 mg/l (mostly as phosphate).

4.5 Chloride and Chlorine

Chloride concentration lowers than 140 mg/l does not create problems regarding the growth of many plants. Table 10 shows the degree of problems experienced by various levels of chloride. The data presented also applies to surface or other irrigation systems where water is absorbed by the root. If water is sprayed on the field and absorbed by the leaves as well, the chloride concentrations of the irrigation water should be below 100 mg/l in order to avoid problems.

13

Chloride level mg/l	Degree of problem
Less than 140	No Problem
Between 140 and 350	Increasing problem
Greater than 350	Severe Problems

Table 10 The degree of problem encountered in various levels of chloride (Bouwer and Idelovitch, 1987)

4.6 Suspended Solids

When suspended solids are deposited onto the soil, they cause a reduction on water infiltration and soil aeration. Because of the biodegradability of most organic solids an oxygen sink is formed on the soil surface which could hinder oxygen movement from the atmosphere into the root zone. Severe deposits of organic solids from sewage effluent on crops and soil, as sometimes-developed in rapid-infiltration basins or other land treatment systems, can actually kill crops. When the sprinkler irrigation system is used, colloidal particles can also be deposited on leaves, where they may reduce photosynthetic activity and adversely affect product appearance. High concentration of suspended solids in the irrigation water may interfere with the flow of water in pipes, sprinklers, drip emitters and hydraulic structures.

Suspended solids, which are mostly of organic nature in sewage effluents, also adversely affect the efficiency of chlorinating. This is because the bacteria and viruses can be protected by organic particles from effective contact with chlorine. Suspended solids also detract from the aesthetics of using sewage effluent from irrigation. This is particularly important in populated areas.

For reasons given above, the removal of suspended solid is necessary before sewage effluent is used for irrigation as much as possible. For unrestricted irrigation, this may require sand filtration or soil aquifer treatments via groundwater recharge to filter the effluent through natural soil, sand and gravel deposits.

4.7 Alkalinity

Due to the high buffering capacity of the soil system, caused by the pH of the irrigation water, the pH of the soil in the root zone is not significantly affected. The main danger connected with water having low or high pH values does not depend on the direct effects of acidity or alkalinity. Instead the direct association of such water with high concentrations of elements such as iron, manganese and aluminum, in the case of acid waters and sodium, carbonates and bicarbonates, in the case of alkaline waters, affect the danger concerned with water.

14

The guidelines and standards present on some of the determinands are summarised in Tables 8, to 19. Table 20 presents standard of water for Irrigation use published by the Departement of Enviroment of Iran (DOE).

Water /soil characteristics	Degree of problem		
	No Problem	Increasing Problem	Severe Problem
Salinity (affects crop water availability) Water salinity EC_w (mmho/cm)	<0.75	0.75-3.0	>3.0
Permeability (affects the infiltration rate into the soil) Water salinity ECw (mmho/cm)	>0.50	0.50-0.20	<0.20
Adj. SAR of water applied to: *			
-Montmorillonite soils	<6	6-9	>9
-Illite Vermiculite soils	<8	8-16	>16
-Kaolinite-sesquioxide soils	<16	16-24	>24
Nitrate's Nitrogen (affects susceptible crops) NO_3-N (or) NH_4-N (mg/l)	<5	5-30	>30

Note:

Adj. SAR means adjusted sodium Adsorption Ratio. ECw means electrical conductivity of Irrigation water.

*.   Values presented are for the dominant type of clay mineral in the soil since structural stability varies between the various clay types. Problems are less likely to develop if water salinity is high; more likely to develop if water salinity is low.

Most tree crops and woody ornamentals are also sensitive to sodium and chloride ions, as are some annual crops.

Table11 Guideline values for interpretation of water quality with regard to salinity, permeability and nitrogen (Ayers and Westcot, 1976)

15

Determinand	Concentration (mg/l)	Determinand	Concentration (mg/l)
Al	5.0	Fe	5.0
As	0.1	Pb	5.0
Be	0.1	Li	(0.075) *
$(HCO_3)^-$	(90) *	Mn	0.2
B	(0.3) *	Mo	0.01
Cd	0.01	Ni	0.2
Cl^-	(70) *	Se	0.02
Cr	0.1	Na	69 mg/l and adj . SAR o f 3
Co	0.05	SO_4^{2-}	(480) *
Cu	0.2	V	0.1
F^-	1.0	Zn	2.0

Note:

No values are available for tungsten, mercury, tin, titanium.

*. The above levels are suitable for all soils and will not affect the plants or the soil. Higher values may be used for a limited period on fine textured neutral to slightly alkaline soil.

**. The values given in brackets are minimum concentrations above which a problem may start to occur   particularly with sensitive crops.

Table 12 Recommended maximum concentrations of phytotoxic elements and other ions in irrigation water (US EPA, 1973; Ayers and Westcot, 1976 and Hart, 1974)

Potential irrigation problem	Units	Degree of restriction on use		
		None	Slight to moderate	Severe
Salinity (Affects crop water availability) EC_{d3w}	ds/m or mmho/cm	0.7	0.7 - 3.0	3.0
TDS	Mg/L	450	450 - 2000	2000
Permeability (affects the infiltration rate of water into soil Evaluate using EC_w and SAR together)				
SAR = 0-3		and ECw 0.7	0.7 - 0.2	0.2
= 3-6		1.2	1.2 - 0.3	0.3
= 6-12		1.9	1.9 - 0.5	0.5
= 12-20		2.9	2.9 - 1.3	1.3
= 20-40		5.0	5.0 - 2.9	2.9
Specific ion toxicity (Affects sensitive crops)				
Sodium (Na)			3 - 9	
Surface irrigation	SAR	3	3	
Sprinkler irrigation	meq/L	3		
Chloride (Cl)	Mg/L	70	70	90
Surface irrigation	meq/L	4	4 - 10	10
	Mg/L	140	140 - 350	350
Sprinkler irrigation	meq/L	3	3	
	Mg/L	100	100	
Boron (B)	Mg/L	0.7	0.7 - 30	3.0
Miscellaneous effects (Affects susceptible crops)				
Nitrogen (total - N)	Mg/L	5	5 - 30	30
Bicarbonate (HCO3) (Overhead sprinkling only)	meq/L	15	1.5 - 8.5	8.5
	Mg/L	90	90 - 500	500
pH	Unit	10	Normal range 6.5 - 8.4	
Residual chlorine (Overhead sprinkling only)	Mg/L		1.0 - 5.0	5.0

Table 13 Guidelines for interpretation of quality for Irrigation (after Westcod and Ayers) after Asano and Pettygrove (1985)

Determinands	For unrestricted irrigation [a] Standards: irrigation	For restricted irrigation [b]
Intestinal nematodes	1 viable egg/l	1 viable egg/l
Faecal coliforms (MPN /100ml)	2.2	MPN 100/100 ml
BOD_5	10.0^c mg/l	20 mg/l
TSS	10.0^d mg/l	20 mg/l
Gr	Absent	

Note:

a.   The concept of unrestricted irrigation refers to use of a high-quality effluent irrigation of all crops on all types of soil in any area during a prolonged period of time, without adverse effect on crops, soils, animals and people involved in the various stages of the agricultural production process and consumers. (Bouwer and Idelovitch, 1987).

b.   The concept of restricted irrigation refers to the use of a low quality effluent only in the specific agricultural area and for specific crops.

c.   Monthly average BOD_5 and TSS concentrations will not exceed 10 mg/l each.

d.   Weekly average BOD_5 and TSS concentrations will not exceed 15 mg/l each.

Monthly average BOD_5 and TSS concentrations for restricted irrigation will not exceed 20 mg/l and faecal coliform organisms MPN 100/100 ml. Weekly average BOD_5 and TSS concentrations will not exceed 30 mg/l and faecal coliform organisms MPN 200/100 ml.

Table 14 Proposed environmental standards for wastewater to be used in Saudi Arabia (Fatwa, 1979)

Suggested treatments achieving the standards in Table 15 are secondary (biological) treatment and disinfecting for categories A-F. Filtration may be required for category G, and chemical coagulation or soil-aquifer treatment may be acceptable category H (Bouwer and Idelovitch, 1987).

Characteristic	Crop and Land-use Category							
	A	B	C	D	E	F	G	H
Ph	4.5-9	4.5-9	4.5-9	6.5-9	4.5-9	4.5-9	4.5-9	4.5-9
Faecal coliforms (CFU/100 ml):								
Geometric mean (5-sample minimum)	1,000	1,000	1,000	1,000	1,000	200	25	2.2
Single sample not to exceed	4,000	4,000	4,000	4,000	2,500	1,000	75	25
Turbidity (NYU)	-	-	-	-	-	-	5	1
Enteric virus (PFU/40 I)	-	-	-	-	-	-	125	1
Entamoeba hystolytica	-	-	-	-	-	-	-	N.D.
Ascaris lumbricoides (roundworm eggs)	-	-	-	-	-	-	N.D.	N.D.
Common large tapeworm	-	-	N.D.	N.D.	-	-	-	-

Note:

CFU = colony-forming unit;

NTU = nephelometer turbidity unity;

PFU = plaque -forming units;

N.D. = none detectable, using; correct samples and methods, and qualified personnel.

The crop and land-use categories are:

A. Orchards.

B. Fodder, seeds, and forages crops.

C. Pastures.

D. Livestock watering.

E. Processed food crops.

F. Landscaped area, restricted access.

G. Landscaped areas, open access.

H. Crops to be consumed raw.

Table 15 Standards for irrigation with reclaimed wastewater in Arizona (Bouwer and Idelovitch, 1987)

Characteristic	Crop Category *			
(1)	I	II	III	IV**
	(1)	(2)	(3)	(4)
Biochemical oxygen demand (mg/l)	60***	45***	35	15
Biochemical oxygen demand filtered	-	-	20	10
Suspended solids content (mg/l)	50***	40	30	15
Total coliforms per 100 ml (80%)	-	-	250	12
Total coliforms per 100 ml (50%)	-	-	-	2.2
Chlorination contact time (Min.)	-	-	60	120
Residual chlorine (mg/l)	-	-	0.15	0.5
Minimum distance from residences (m)	300	250	-	-
Minimum distance form paved roads	30	25	-	-

Note:

* . All values refer to the 80 - percentile, except for total coliforms in category IV, where the 50 - percentile is also specified.

** . Unrestricted irrigation; sand filtration of the effluent is mandatory.

*** . Not applicable to effluent form oxidation ponds with detention time of more than 15 days, where most BOD_5 and suspended solids are of algal origin.

Table 16 Standards for irrigation with reclaimed wastewater in Israel (Bouwer and Idelovitch, 1987)

Irrigation use (1)	Treatment required (2)	Maximum total coliforms per 100 ml (3)	Other (4)
Fodder, seed, Forest crop	Primary *, disinfection	230	Settleable solids, 5 ml litter/hr storage for one week
Pasture for dairy animals	Secondary, disinfection	23	
Golf courses, cemeteries, lawns, playgrounds	Secondary, disinfection	23	
Orchards, vineyards (surface irrigation only)	Secondary, disinfection	23	
Food crops (surface irrigation only)	Secondary, disinfection	23	
Food crops (surface irrigation only)	Secondary, disinfection	23 No sample exceeds 23 in a 30 day period	Turbidity $\leq$ 2 TU

Note:

* The standard for primary treatment is a reduction of BOD by 35 % and of suspended solids by 55 %.

Table 17   Wastewater Standards for Irrigation in State of Washington (AWWA, 1985)

Irrigation of crop types (1)	Health criteria @ (2)	Primary treatment (3)	Secondary treatment (4)	Sand filtration or equivalent polishing methods (5)	Disinfection (6)
Crops not for direct human consumption	A+D	***			
Crops eaten cooked, fish-culture	B+D or C+D	***	***	*	*
Crops eaten raw	C+D	***	***	*	***

@ Health criteria:

A= Freedom from gross solids; significant removal of parasite eggs;

B= As A, plus significant removal of bacteria;

C= Not more than 100 coliform organisms per 100 ml in 80 % of samples;

D= No chemicals that lead to undesirable residues in crops or fish.

Note: In order to meet the given health criteria, processes marked *** will be essential.

In addition, processes marked * may sometimes be required.

Table 18 Suggested Treatment Processes to Meet Given Health Criteria for Wastewater Reuse by WHO, 1973

Trace element (1)	Permanent irrigation of all soils (2)	Up to 20 yr. irrigation of fine-textured neutral to alkaline soils (pH 6-8.5) (3)
Al	5	20
As	0.1	2
Be	0.1	0.5
B - sensitive crops	0.75	2
semitolerant crops	1	
Tolerant crops	2	
Cd	0.01	0.05
Cr	0.1	1
Co	0.05	5
Cu	0.2	5
F^-	1	15
Fe	5	20
Pb	5	10
Li : citrus	0.075	0.075
Other crops	2.5	2.5
Mn	0.2	10
Mo	0.01	0.05
Ni	0.2	2
Se	0.02	0.02
V	0.1	1
Zn	2	10

Table 19 Recommended maximum limits (mg/l) for trace elements in irrigation water (Bouwer and Idelovitch, 1987)

23

Constituent	Long-Term Use (Mg/L)	Short-Term Use (Mg/L)	Remarks
Aluminum	5.0	20	Can cause nonproductivity in acid soils, but soils at pH 5.5 to 8.0 will precipitate the ion and eliminate toxicity
Arsenic	0.10	2.0	Toxicity to plant varies widely, ranging from 12 mg/L for Sudan grass to less than 0.05 mg/l for rice
Beryllium	0.10	0.5	Toxicity to plants varies widely, ranging from 5 mg/L for kale to 0.5 mg/L for bush beans.
Boron	0.75	2.0	Essential to plant growth, with optimum yields for many obtained in a few-tenths mg/L in nutrient Solutions. Toxic to many sensitive plants (e.g., Citrus) at 1 mg/L. Usually sufficient quantities in reclaimed water to correct soil deficiencies. Most grasses relatively at 2.0 to 10 mg/L.
Cadmium	0.01	0.05	Toxic to beans beets, and turnips at concentrations as low as 0.1 mg/L in nutrient solution. Conservative limits recommended.

Table 19*A* Recommended limits for constituents in Reclaimed Water for Irrigation (EPA, 1992) Cont. /d…

Constituent	Long-Term Use (Mg/L)	Short -Term Use (Mg/L)	Remarks
Chromium	0.1	1.0	Not generally recognized as an essential growth element. Conservative limits recommended due to lack of knowledge on the toxicity to plants.
Cobalt	0.05	5.0	Toxic to tomato plants at 0.1 mg/l in nutrient solution. Tends to be inactivated by neutral and alkaline soils.
Copper	0.2	5.0	Toxic to a number of plants at 0.1 to 1.0 mg/L in nutrient solution.
Fluoride	1.0	15.0	Inactivated by neutral and alkaline soils.
Iron	5.0	20.0	Not toxic to plants in aerated soils, but can contribute to soil acidification and loss of essential phosphorus and molybdenum.
Lead	5.0	10.0	Can inhibit plant cell growth at very high concentrations.
Lithium	2.5	2.5	Tolerated by most crops at up to 5 mg/L, mobile in soil. Toxic to citrus at low doses, recommended limit is 0.075 mg/L
Manganese	0.2	10.0	Toxic to a number of crops at a few-tenths to a few mg/L in acid soils.

Table 19A   Continued

Constituent	Long-Term Use (Mg/L)	Short -Term Use (Mg/L)	Remarks
Molybdenum	0.01	0.05	Nontoxic to plants at normal concentrations in soil and water. Can be toxic to livestock if forage is grown in soils with high levels of available molybdenum
Nickel	0.2	2.0	Toxic to a number of plants at 0.5 to 1.0 mg/L; reduced toxicity at neutral or alkaline pH.
Selenium	0.02	0.02	Toxic to plants at low concentrations and to livestock if forage is grown in soils with low levels of added selenium.
Tin, Tungsten, & Titanium	---	---	Effectively excluded by plants; specific tolerance levels unknown
Vanadium	0.1	1.0	Toxic to many plants at relatively low concentrations.
Zinc	2.0	10.0	Toxic to many plants at widely varying concentrations; reduced toxicity at increased pH (6 or above) and in fine-textured or organic soils.

Table 19A   *Continued*

Constituent	Recommended Limit	Remarks
pH	6.0	Most effects of pH on plant growth are indirect (e.g., pH effects on heavy metals' toxicity)
TDS	500-2000 mg/L	Below 500 mg/L, no detrimental effects are usually noticed. Between 500 and 1000 mg/L TDS in irrigation water can affect sensitive plants. At 1000 to 2000 mg/L TDS levels can affect many crops and careful management practices should be followed. Above 2000 mg/L water can be used regularly only for tolerant plants on permeable soils
Free Chlorine Residual	< 1 mg/L	

Table 19B   Recommended Limits for Constituents in Reclaimed Water for irrigation (EPA, 1992)

No.	Pollution determinands	Irrigation uses mg/l
1	Al	5
2	Ba	1
3	Be	0.5
4	B	1
5	Cd	0.05
6	Ca	--
7	cr^{+3}	1
8	cr	1
9	Co	0.05
10	Cu	0.2
11	Li	2.5
12	Mg	100
13	Mn	1
14	Hg	0
15	Mo	0.01
16	Ni	0.2
17	Fe	3
18	Pb	1
19	Se	0.1
20	Ag	0.1
21	Zn	2
22	V	0.1
23	Radio- Active Material	0
24	AS	0.1
25	Si	0.2

Table 20   The maximum standard levels of pollution can discharge into various accepting sources (from the DOE, 1994).   Cont./d...

No.	Pollution determinands	Irrigation uses mg/l
26	Cl^-	600
27	F	2
28	p	-
29	Cn	0.1
30	C_6H_5OH	1
31	CH_2O	1
32	NH_4-N	-
33	NO_2	-
34	NO_3	-
35	SO_4^{2-}	500
36	SO_3^{2-}	1
37	TSS	100
38	Settelable	-
39	TSS	0
40	TDS	**
41	Oil	10
42	BOD	100
43	COD	200
44	DO	2
45	MBAS	0.5
46	Turbidity	50
47	Colour	75
48	T	***
49	pH	6 -8.5
50	Faecal Coliform	400/100 ml
51	MPN	1000/100 ml
52	Intestinal nematodes	1 Viable egg/l

Table 20 Continued

Some selected guidelines and standards for the use of water for agricultural purposes were outlined previously. These included American (Arizona), Saudi Arabia, Israeli, EC, EPA and WHO standards. The Iranian standard as well as the result of some of the researchers in this field is presented as guidelines. They are shown in Tables 7, 8 and 10 to 20.

Usually, standards are prepared according to the countries climatic conditions, and the type of the crops considered. For example, by considering the table for the Arizona (Table 15), in order to minimize the danger for the public health and reduce the costs, eight different groups are involved depending on the type of the crop considered.

Table 16, representing the case for Israel, which illustrates four groups, it will not be economical if the same level of treatment is considered for all agricultural products. Even the Saudis Arabian standard encloses two groups. Also in Iran, considering the climatic conditions of the different parts of the country and the type of crops to be harvested, the standard should be modified. However as can be seen in Table 20, the Environmental Protection Institute has only a single standard for all parts of the country and for all the crops, making the treatment process very uneconomical.

The researcher suggests that the Ministry of Energy which is responsible for water authorities together with Ministry of Agriculture and Rural Development, they should help the Ministry of Health, Treatment and Medical, Education in developing a standard which considers, at least, the four different climates present in the country. Water types used for agricultural purposes can be considered for each subgrouping. In this manner an economic policy can be developed which, not only provides suitable water for the various usages, but also it is safe for plant consumers. Another shortage, which was felt, regards the number of the helminth eggs which is considered since 1994. However, the World Bank study of enhanced wastewater treatment suggested that a treatment technology is required which achieves: maximum removal of helminth eggs (Feachem and Blum, 1984).

The importance of helminth eggs to the general well being is vital. The results collected by the TRWA on this determinand, measured at station 7 over a period of four months, and collected four times daily are analysed and presented in Table 21. Thus the concentrations of some of the helminth eggs numbers (Strongyloidiae and Ascaris) are above the standard ones illustrated in Tables 14 and 15. Ascaris lumbricoides cause roundworm infection in warm climates (Feachem and Blum, 1984). (At least there is a five month warm period in Tehran.) Strongyloidiae cause Helminthic infection. Comparison shows that the number of helminth eggs downstream of the network is twelve times higher than those of the Saudi Arabian or local standards. They are shown in Tables 14 and 20. Strong measures should be sought in order to limit these levels in the network, especially from known sources such as treatment plants which discharge treated effluents into the streams under the study in this research. Dolatabad, (a small town in downstream shown in Figure 1), is one of many points where discharged treatment effluents enter into the streams without any treatment. Hence the usage of this water for agricultural purposes may cause problems. The known related illnesses, especially for those that work on farms or consume their raw products are presented in a tabulated form in Appendix A.

The water existing in the network appears to be hazardous to the public health. The level of MPN test for total coliforms with no dilution showed 2400 per 100 ml. But when the sample was diluted 10000 times, the MPN test shows a value of 9.2×10^6. This is shown in Table 22. This number indicates the pathogen germ existence in the water. Compared to the relevant standards, this is an alarming figure which may also be seen from the ratio of the numbers of total coliforms in station 7 to that of the Iranian standard is 9.2 (10^3. The Iranian standard is shown in Table 20. Also, considering other passed data for TRWA determinands such as BOD_5 it is clear that its level is much higher than other standards shown in Tables 14 and 16, however, this is an acceptable limit with local standard (The DOE). Tables 23 to 25 show the result of one-year experimental work. They are necessary for comparison with international or local standard for agricultural purposes. Table 26 illustrates some important determinands in crop cultivating.

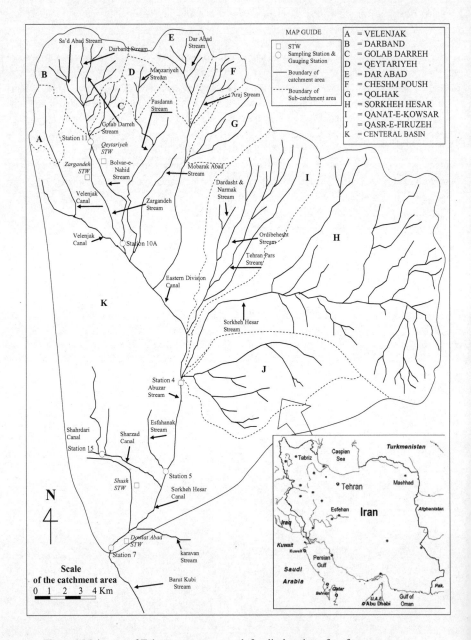

Figure 1 Main part of Tehran streams network for discharging of surface water.

		30.07 99	11.08 99	18.08 99	25.08 99	27.08 99	01.09 99	03.09 99	20.09 99	29.09 99	22.10 99	29.10 99	06.11 99	17.11 99	24.11 99
HOCK WORM	MAX.	0.0	0.0	0.0	0.0	0.0	0.0	0.0	0.0	0.0	0.0	0.0	0.0	0.0	1.0
	MEAN	0.0	0.0	0.0	0.0	0.0	0.0	0.0	0.0	0.0	0.0	0.0	0.0	0.0	0.25
	MIN.	0.0	0.0	0.0	0.0	0.0	0.0	0.0	0.0	0.0	0.0	0.0	0.0	0.0	0.0
ASCARIS-LUMBRICODIES	MAX.	0.0	10	0.0	0.0	10	0.0	0.0	0.0	0.0	0.0	0.0	10	0.0	0.0
	MEAN	0.0	2.5	0.0	0.0	2.756	0.0	0.0	0.0	0.0	0.0	0.0	2.5	0.0	0.0
	MIN.	0.0	0.0	0.0	0.0	0.0	0.0	0.0	0.0	0.0	0.0	0.0	0.0	0.0	0.0
STRONGYLOIDE-STERCORALIS	MAX.	0.0	0.0	0.0	1	20	0.0	5	0.0	12	0.0	0.0	10	10	10
	MEAN	0.0	0.0	0.0	0.25	6	0.0	1.5	0.0	8.25	0.0	0.0	3	2.75	2.5
	MIN.	0.0	0.0	0.0	0.0	0.0	0.0	0.0	0.0	0.0	0.0	0.0	0.0	0.0	0.0
HYMENOLEPIS-NANA	MAX.	0.0	0.0	0.0	1	0.0	0.0	0.0	0.0	0.0	0.0	0.0	0.0	10	0.0
	MEAN	0.0	0.0	0.0	0.25	0.0	0.0	0.0	0.0	0.0	0.0	0.0	0.0	2.5	0.0
	MIN.	0.0	0.0	0.0	0.0	0.0	0.0	0.0	0.0	0.0	0.0	0.0	0.0	0.0	0.0
ENTEROBIUS-VERMICULARIS	MAX.	0.0	0.0	0.0	0.0	0.0	0.0	0.0	0.0	0.0	0.0	0.0	0.0	0.0	0.0
	MEAN	0.0	0.0	0.0	0.0	0.0	0.0	0.0	0.0	0.0	0.0	0.0	0.0	0.0	0.0
	MIN.	0.0	0.0	0.0	0.0	0.0	0.0	0.0	0.0	0.0	0.0	0.0	0.0	0.0	0.0
TRICHURIS-TRICHIURA	MAX.	0.0	0.0	0.0	0.0	0.0	0.0	0.0	0.0	0.0	0.0	0.0	1	0.0	0.0
	MEAN	0.0	0.0	0.0	0.0	0.0	0.0	0.0	0.0	0.0	0.0	0.0	0.25	0.0	0.0
	MIN.	0.0	0.0	0.0	0.0	0.0	0.0	0.0	0.0	0.0	0.0	0.0	0.0	0.0	0.0

Table 21   The levels of helminth eggs measured by TRWA at Station 7 (Figure , 1)

33

Time of sampling	Station	Number of times diluted	Combination of positives	MPN Index /100 ml
Jun. 13,99	10A	_____	5-5-5	>>2400
Aug.1, 99	11	_____	5-5-5	>>2400
Aug.1, 99	14	_____	5-0-0	23
Aug.17, 99	4	_____	5-5-5	>>2400
Aug. 17, 99	5	_____	5-5-5-	>>2400
Aug.26, 99	3	2000	5-5-5	>$4.8*10^6$
Aug.26, 99	3B	2000	5-5-5	>$4.8*10^6$
Sept.5, 99	5	3000	5-5-5	>$7.2*10^6$
Sept.5, 99	15	3000	5-5-5	>$7.2*10^6$
Nov.14, 99	7	5000	5-5-3	$4.6*10^6$
Nov.14,99	15	5000	5-5-5	>$12*10^6$
Nov.23, 99	4	5000	5-5-5	>$12*10^6$
Nov.13, 99	5	5000	5-5-2	>$2.7*10^6$
Sept.,3 99	3	7000	5-5-3	$6.44*10^6$
Sept.3, 99	3B	7000	5-5-0	$1.68*10^6$
Dec.19, 99	5	7000	5-5-0	$1.68*10^6$
Dec.19, 99	15	7000	5-5-2	$3.78*10^6$

Table 22 The levels of total coliforms measured in this research work at various stations Cont./d...

Time of sampling	Station	Number of times diluted	Combination of positives	MPN Index /100 ml
Mar.3, 00	4	7000	5-5-0	$1.68*10^6$
Mar.3, 00	5	7000	5-5-0	$1.68*10^6$
May 14, 00	7	7000	5-5-3	$6.44*10^6$
May 14, 00	15	7000	5-5-5	$16.8*10^6$
July 29,00	7	7000	5-5-3	$6.44*10^6$
July29, 00	15	7000	5-5-5	$>16.8*10^6$
Aug.11, 00	7	10000	5-4-1	$1.7*10^6$
Aug. 11,00	15	10000	4-2-0	$0.22*10^6$
Sept.1, 00	7	7000	5-5-2	$3.78*10^6$
Sept.,1 00	15	7000	5-5-5	$>16.8*10^6$
Sept.15, 00	7	7000	5-5-4	$11.2*10^6$
Sept.15, 00	15	7000	5-5-5	$>16.8*10^6$
Sept.29, 00	7	7000	5-5-3	$6.44*10^6$
Sept.29, 00	15	7000	5-5-5	$>16.8*10^6$
Oct.21, 00	7	8000	5-5-3	$7.36*10^6$
Oct. 21,00	15	8000	5-5-4	$12.8*10^6$
Nov.11, 00	7	8000	5-5-5	$>19.2*10^6$
Nov. 11,00	15	8000	5-5-3	$7.36*10^6$
Feb.25, 00	7	10000	5-5-3	$9.2*10^6$
Feb. 25,2001	15	10000	5-5-3	$2.8*10^6$

Table 22 Continued

Period	Wet Season			Dry Season		
Range of result	Max.	Av.	Min.	Max.	Av.	Min.
T (C°)	36.00	12.00	0.00	38.00	29.17	14.00
DO (%)	8.10	6.34	0.00	5.70	3.02	0.40
pH (-)	9.00	7.78	6.80	9.80	8.34	7.10
BOD_5 (mg/l)	125.00	43.77	10.00	140.00	66.32	34.00
BOD_7 (mg/l)	155.00	52.73	16.00	170.00	78.64	44.00
COD (mg/l)	237.00	62.31	10.00	920.00	163.00	42.00
NH_4-N (mg/l)	5.30	2.29	0.50	7.37	3.42	1.05
NO_3^- (mg/l)	9.70	6.23	2.30	8.12	4.86	0.30
NO_2^- (mg/l)	2.00	0.39	0.01	1.60	0.69	0.05
ON (m^3/sec)	15.40	6.39	0.60	160.00	12.70	2.00
TN (mg/l)	26.25	15.32	6.80	34.25	18.66	7.75
TSS (mg/l)	988.00	300.10	40.00	844.00	325.80	40.00
VS (mg/l)	438.00	119.90	30.00	960.00	172.90	40.00
Inorganic (mg/l)	996.00	192.90	8.00	688.00	187.50	0.00
Set.S (mg/l)	40.00	2.99	0.70	10.00	2.42	0.50
Gr (mg/l)	201.00	77.16	20.00	120.00	62.83	10.00
Det (mg/l)	7.22	2.05	0.50	7.00	2.67	0.30
SO_4^{2-} (mg/l)	2.60	0.29	0.00	2.97	0.75	0.13
PO_4^{3-} (mg/l)	3.80	1.20	0.00	6.00	1.87	0.00
Cd (mg/l)	0.10	0.06	0.02	0.08	0.05	0.00
Cr (mg/l)	0.07	0.01	0.00	0.38	0.03	0.00
Cu (mg/l)	0.42	0.10	0.01	0.38	0.07	0.00
Pb (mg/l)	0.20	0.12	0.00	0.55	0.09	0.00
Ni (m^3/sec)	0.16	0.07	0.01	0.20	0.05	0.00
Zn (mg/l)	56.00	24.08	0.12	0.93	0.27	0.10
Al (mg/l)	35.37	8.24	0.00	24.00	3.34	0.05
Fe (mg/l)	57.50	8.39	0.00	15.00	4.78	0.80
HCO_3^{2-} (mg/l)	397.72	322.00	200.00	402.60	336.72	268.40
Na (mg/l)	40.00	18.00	11.00	22.20	18.70	16.00

Dry season includes June, July, August, September and October,

The wet season includes November, December, January, February, March, April and May

Table 23 One year experimental work from 6/97 to 6/98 for station 7 (Morning)

Period	Dry Season		
Range of result	Max.	Av.	Min.
T (C^o)	40.00	32.00	14.00
DO (%)	5.70	2.88	0.00
pH(-)	8.50	7.69	7.50
BOD$_5$ (mg/l)	106.00	57.48	30.00
BOD$_7$ (mg/l)	120.00	73.71	30.00
COD (mg/l)	168.00	89.18	48.00
NH$_4$-N (mg/l)	4.40	1.73	0.35
NO$_3^-$ (mg/l)	6.37	3.61	0.25
NO$_2^-$ (mg/l)	1.60	0.49	0.04
ON (m^3/sec)	10.60	5.70	0.80
TN (mg/l)	26.25	12.47	4.95
TSS (mg/l)	868.00	349.50	104.00
VS (mg/l)	276.00	152.00	56.00
Inorganic (mg/l)	836.00	237.90	8.00
Set.S (mg/l)	5.50	2.20	0.00
Gr (mg/l)	200.00	68.39	0.00
Det (mg/l)	9.00	4.98	0.00
SO$_4^{2-}$ (mg/l)	9.79	0.73	0.00
PO$_4^{3-}$ (mg/l)	7.60	2.69	0.00
Cd (mg/l)	0.09	0.06	0.40
Cr (mg/l)	0.30	0.04	0.00
Cu (mg/l)	0.25	0.06	0.00
Pb (mg/l)	0.37	0.10	0.00
Ni (m^3/sec)	0.70	0.10	0.00
Zn (mg/l)	1.08	0.28	0.10
Al (mg/l)	65.50	9.01	0.04
Fe (mg/l)	38.75	6.41	0.63

Table 24 One year experimental work from 6/97 to 6/98 for station 7 (Figure 1) (Afternoon)

Period	Dry Season		
Range of result	Max.	Av.	Min.
T (C°)	28.00	18.90	6.00
DO (%)	6.70	4.86	0.00
pH(-)	8.60	7.87	7.30
BOD_5 (mg/l)	62.00	34.20	10.00
BOD_7 (mg/l)	78.00	48.13	25.00
COD (mg/l)	92.00	53.08	13.00
NH_4-N (mg/l)	6.15	0.95	0.15
NO_3^- (mg/l)	9.00	5.71	1.30
NO_2^- (mg/l)	1.60	0.40	0.08
ON (m^3/Sec)	14.40	5.51	0.00
TN (mg/l)	58.38	13.65	0.75
TSS (mg/l)	812.00	217.20	32.00
VS (mg/l)	488.00	105.50	12.00
Inorganic (mg/l)	628.00	113.60	0.00
Set.S (mg/l)	3.00	0.87	0.10
Gr (mg/l)	140.00	60.78	20.00
Det (mg/l)	6.40	2.54	0.40
SO_4^{2-} (mg/l)	1.41	0.32	0.00
PO_4^{3-} (mg/l)	3.80	1.58	0.50
Cd (mg/l)	0.09	0.05	0.00
Cr (mg/l)	0.10	0.01	0.00
Cu (mg/l)	0.38	0.05	0.00
Pb (mg/l)	0.34	0.08	0.00
Ni (m^3/sec)	0.11	0.04	0.00
Zn (mg/l)	1.50	0.26	0.26
Al (mg/l)	7.10	2.32	2.32
Fe (mg/l)	12.00	3.45	3.45

Table 25 One year experimental work from 6/97 to 6/98 for station 7 (Night)

Period	Wet Season			Dry Season		
Range of result	Max.	Av.	Min.	Max.	Av.	Min.
Ca (mg/l)	105.00	84.53	68.10	96.00	78.51	35.20
Mg (mg/l)	27.64	18.65	11.17	45.46	20.33	4.38
Na (mg/l)	40.00	18.00	11.00	22.20	18.70	16.00
SO_4^{2-} (mg/l)	2.60	2.97	0.00	2.97	0.29	0.13
HCO_3^{2-} (mg/l)	397.72	322.00	200.00	402.60	336.72	268.40

Table 26   Sampling results for station seven in this research

Using forecast data obtained from developed models described (asadollahfardi,2003) for station 7(Figure 1) which were compared them with local standard (DOE) as shown in Table 20 it can be concluded that no problem is caused for some determinands such as DO, pH, CL, COD, other determinands such as TDS, TSS may cause slight to moderate problems for agricultural usage's. This is shown in Table 27. For example the amount of total suspended solids is higher than what is prescribed in the standard. As mentioned before, the above level of TSS causes problems to the crop's roots.

This book demonstrated that, first, local standard has some deficits in the definitions. For example no standards are available for NH_4-N, TS, Ca and nutrient in concentration. Some other standards for certain determinands have not been reasonably defined such as COD, DO as shown in Table 20. Secondly, forecast values shown in Table 27 are mean values, however the comparison carried out in this research has given a quality baseline for the water used in agricultural usage.

Determinand	Season	Station No 7 Forecast data	Local standard Irrigation uses (DOE)	Degree of restriction on usage
pH	Wet	7.56	6-8.5	
	Dry	7.56	6-8.5	None
TDS	Wet	557.43 mg/l	450-2000*	Slight to
	Dry	626.89 "	450-2000*	Moderate
CL	Wet	78.28 "	250	
	Dry	89.122 "	250	None
COD	Wet	137.23 "	200	
	Dry	136.37 "	200	None
TSS	Wet	126.86 "	100	Slight to
	Dry	157.53 "	100	Moderate
DO	Wet	5.28 "	2	
	Dry	3.08 "	2	None
COND	Wet	853.75 "	1650	
	Dry	1124.65 "	1650	None

Note:
    * This standard was in old local standard.

Table 27 Comparison of mean values of the forecast data from the developed model (Asaollahfardi, 2002) for station 7 with existing local standard.

As a result of the comparison between Table 27 and Table 28, it is revealed that the degree of restriction on use for two standards is slightly different.

The principal chemical characteristics of the effluent which determine its suitability for irrigation usage are the salinity which may be defined as or the total concentration of dissolved solids (TDS), sodium absorption, ratio (SAR), residual sodium carbonate concentration, substances and metals found in low or trace concentrations and nutrient concentrations (Cowan and Johnson, 1984).

Determinand	Season	Station No 7 forecast data (mean values)	Other standard Table 7.13	Degree of restriction on use
pH	Wet	7.56	6.5- 8.5	
	Dry	7.56	6.5- 8.4	None
NH₄-N	Wet	8.55 mg/l	<5*	Slight to
	Dry	7.51 "	<5*	moderate
TDS	Wet	557.43 "	450-2000	Slight to
	Dry	626.89 "	450-2000	moderate
CL	Wet	78.28 "	70	Slight to
	Dry	89.122 "	70	moderate

Note:

   * This standard is obtained from table 11.

Table 28 Comparison of some data, which obtained from the developed models (Asadollahfardi, 2002) for station 7 with standard in Table 13

Salinity is measured by electrical conductivity (EC) as mentioned before. Irrigation water with an EC of 1650 mmho/cm or greater is defined as having high salinity. Unfortunately local standard does not provide any measurements for salinity. However the value of 1650 in this study is used for comparison purposes.

High concentrations of sodium ions can cause a progressive deterioration in soil particles causing a decrease in the hydraulic conductivity, aeration and a consequent build up of salinity (Cowan and Johnson, 1984). Table 29 illustrates the comparison between the amounts of some determinands, which are important in agricultural purposes with local standard. This comparison concludes that there is no significant problem in the chemical constituent.

The result of total dissolved solid (TDS) and HCO_3^{--} from experimental work, shows that the values relating to the standard value is rather high and this is considered as a slight to moderate problem. The concentration of some trace elements such as Ni, pb, Cu and Zn are not above the standard of water for agricultural use as shown in Table 29.

The ratio of SAR, which is an important parameter in growing the crops, is less than three, which is not a major problem for growing crops.

Determinand	Season	Station No 7 Passed data	Local standard (DOE) mg/l	Restriction on use
Mg	Wet	18.65	100	
	Dry	20.33	100	None
COND	Wet		1650*	
	Dry		1650*	None
HCO_3^{--}	Wet	322	90-500	slight to
	Dry	336.72	90-500	moderate
SAR	Wet	2.51	3	
	Dry	2.66	3	None
TDS	Wet	557.43	450-2000	slight to
	Dry	626.89	450-2000	moderate
Ni	Wet	0.07	0.2	
	Dry	0.05	0.2	None
Pb	Wet	0.12	1	
	Dry	0.09	1	None
Cu	Wet	0.1	0.2	
	Dry	0.05	0.2	None
Zn	Wet	-	2	
	Dry	0.27	2	None
helminth	Wet	12	1	Severe
Eggs	Dry	12	1	Problem
Coliforms	Wet	1.7×10^6	1000	Severe
	Dry	1.7×10^6	1000	Problem

Note:
    * This is not existing in local standard.

Table 29 Comparison of some passed data at station 7 with local standard

The DOE has prohibited the use of such water for irrigation of raw consumed vegetation and crops. This water which flows from about six to ten kilometers, from station 7 moves with a low speed allowing the settlement of suspended solids. The low speed allowing the water flow would assist in the decrease of helminth eggs. The process resembles the stabilization pond. The types of crops that cultivate with this water are wheat, alfalfas, corn for animal and barley. The texture of the soil consists of clay with a small amount of sand. Most crops can be cultivated in this area, however farmers prefer using cultivated Alfalfa and corn for animal consumption, as it is easier for them to sell these types of crops with high price. Table 18 suggests the treatment processes which meets given health criteria for wastewater reuse by WHO. It is clear that at the present time two types of crops cultivated with this water need primary treatment (A+D), however wheat and barley need higher treatment than the two types of crops mentioned in Table 18.

5.   Methods of water quality improvement for agricultural purposes

As a result of the existing high level of helminth eggs in station seven which is shown in Table 21, the most important hazard to the public health is helminthic diseases. These types of diseases may be epidemic for some reasons, one of which uses this water for irrigation. World Health Organisation (1989) recommended guidelines for safe use of wastewater in agriculture, which is shown in Table 30. In Table 30 there are three categories, showing a separate standard for each group.

There are some strategies to control pollution as a result of polluted water used in agriculture, which are as follows:

1)   Treatment of polluted water

2)   Crop restriction

3)   Human exposure control

4)   Appropriate application of sewage techniques

From the above mentioned strategy only full treatment can completely remove all the potential risks from consumers of plants and crops. Adopting crop restriction as a means of health protection in reusing schemes will require a strong institutional framework. It also requires the capacity to monitor and control and also comply with regulations and methods of enforcing them. Farmers must be informed of the reason for which such crop restriction is necessary and appropriate assistance should be given in developing a balanced mix of crops, which makes full use of the partially treated wastewater available. They may also need assistance with marketing (WHO, 1989). Crop restriction is a strategy for the protection of the consuming public however it does not provide protection to the farm workers and their families where a low quality effluent is used in irrigation (Mara and Cairncross 1989). Protection by means of wearing of protective clothing and maintaining high levels of hygiene and possibly immunization against, or chemotherapeutic control of selected infections can be considered as temporary palliative measures.

Category	Reuse conditions	Exposed group	Intestinal nematodes [b] (arithmetic mean no. of eggs per litre [c])	Faecal coliforms (geometric mean no. per 100 ml [c])	Wastewater treatment expected to achieve the required microbiological quality
A	Irrigation of crops likely to be eaten uncooked, sports fields, public parks [d]	Workers, consumers, public	≤1	≤1000 [d]	A series of stabilisation ponds designed to achieves the microbiological quality indicated, or equivalent treatment
B	Irrigation of cereal crops, industrial crops, fodder crops, pasture and trees [e]	Workers	≤1	No standard recommended	Retention in stabilisation ponds for 8-10 days or equivalent helminth and faecal coliform removal
C	Localised irrigation of crops in category B if exposure of workers and the public does not occur	None	Not applicable	Not applicable	Pre-treatment as required by the irrigation technology, but not less than primary sedimentation

a) In specific cases, local epidemiological, sociocultural and environmental factors should be taken into account, and the guidelines modified accordingly.

b) Ascaris and Trichuris species and hookworms.

c) During the irrigation period.

d) A more stringent guideline (≤200 faecal coliforms per 100 ml) is appropriate for public lawns, such as hotel lawns, with which the public may come into direct contact.

e) In the case of fruit trees, irrigation should cease two weeks before fruit is picked, and no fruit should be picked off the ground. Sprinkler irrigation should not be used.

Table 30 Recommended microbiological quality guidelines for wastewater use in agriculture (WHO, 1989)

Lopez et al (2002) applied the membrane filtration, simplified treatments, storage reservoirs and constructed wetlands technologies to evaluate suitability of them to treat municipal wastewater for agricultural irrigation. Their results showed that the following :

1- In the membrane filtration the microbial quality of treated effluents was higher than that of local well-water employed for irrigation
2- In the basic treatment in order to keep the agronomic potential of organic matter and nutrients present in urban wastewater, olive trees were irrigated with effluents produced by skipping biological processes and this resulted in a yield increase of 50%; storage reservoirs — TSS, BOD5, COD and nutrients concentrations attained the in force Italian limits for WW agricultural reuse
3- The constructed wetlands — evidenced average efficiencies for TSS, BOD5, COD, TN and TP removals were 85%, 65%, 75%, 42% and 32% respectively.

Al Salem and Abouzaid (2006) stated a few suggestions for reaching full use of reclaimed wastewater and maintain human health which as follows:

- All wastewater should be treated and utilize the entire quantity in a suitable context. Merely high-value agricultural products should be farmed and water should be assigned to uses that have the maximum worth and prevent contamination.
- The current limits on wastewater reuse related to their country should be reviewed and decided how to conquer them by the policy –makers and experienced experts.
- Inducements for conservation should be presented and sanctions/ fines for unreasonable use should be obliged. Consumers should meet the cost of the economic water price; this will help avoid the uneconomical use/reuse of water.
- Considering the priorities, water plans, strategies and investments for the long-term should be making a decision with the participation of beneficiaries'. Reclaimed water should not be released into the sea as it is a waste of this precious water resource.
- Wastewater reuse guidelines should bring up to date to match recently gained knowledge and a complete approach should be employed for health protection measures not conditional on the treatment measure as the only method for health protection
- Wastewater reuse projects should be designed as an integral fraction of the wastewater network and water resources plans.

Police et al. (2004) studied a 2-year field examination of municipal treated wastewater for the irrigation of tomato and fennel in Southern Italy. Just about 500 m3 of tertiary membrane filtered wastewater with no additional disinfection was provided with one of two parcels (500 m2 each) of an examination field. The second package was moderately watered with 500 m3 of conventional healthy ground water. For two years experimental works,, the pilot plant performance consequence was great in terms of suspended solids and removal of bacteria.

Referring to the farming outcome, no considerable dissimilarity was viewed after 2 years, both in terms of microbiological quality of the crops and characteristics of the soil. Their entire consequences were showed the membrane filtered municipal effluent as a practical choice of water resource for irrigation.

Capra and Scicolo (2004) studied with experimental examinations on the performance of six types of filters (gravel media, disk and screen) and the four sorts of drip emitters (vortex and labyrinth) utilizing five kinds of municipal wastewater that have not experienced before advanced treatment. The labyrinth emitters less sensitive to clogging than vortex emitters. The gravel media filter certain the best performance; however, the disc filter, which is cheaper and easier to manage, guaranteed performance like to that of the gavel media filter. The examination demonstrated the significance of the technology employed in manufacturing disk filters. Screen filters were revealed to be inappropriate for use with wastewater, with the exception of diluted and settled wastewater. They found that the theoretical Discharge of filters, proposed by the manufacturers for clean water, is not sufficient for wastewater of the type used in the trials (suspended solids greater than 78 mg/l and BOD5 more than 25 mg/l of O2

Irrigation water, including treated wastewater, can be applied to the land in the five following general methods (WHO, 1989):

a) By flooding: almost all the land surface is watered;

b) By means of furrows: only part of the ground surface is watered;

c) By means of sprinkler: the soil and crops are watered in much the same way as they are by rainfall;

d) By subsurface irrigation: the surface is only slightly watered, if at all, but the subsoil is saturated; and

e) By means of localized (trickle, drip or bubblier) irrigation; water is applied to the root zone of each individual plant at an adjustable rate.

Flooding needs minimum investment, but probably exposes field workers to the greatest risk. Sprinkler irrigation should not be used on vegetables and fruit unless the effluent meets the guideline for category A conditions, (Table 30), and flood irrigation should not be used for vegetables (WHO, 1989).

The five irrigation methods mentioned for irrigation have advantages and disadvantages illustrated in Table 31.

Irrigation method	Factors affecting choice	Special measures for wastewater
Border (flooding) Irrigation	Low cost, exact levelling not required	Thorough protection for field workers, crop-handlers and consumers
Furrow irrigation	Low cost, levelling may be needed	Protection for field workers, possibly for crop-handlers and consumers
Sprinkler irrigation	Medium water use efficiency, levelling not required	Some Category B crops, especially tree fruit, should not be grown. Minimum distance 50-100m from houses and roads.
Subsurface and localised irrigation	High cost, high water use efficiency, higher yields	Anaerobic wastes should not be used because of odour nuisance. Filtration to prevent clogging of emitters.

Table31   Factors affecting choice of irrigation method, and special measures required when wastewater is used

A combination of the mentioned strategies may be used for a more desirable requirement, which are shown in Figure 2.

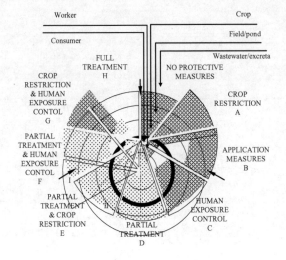

I) Pond treatment) Conventional treatment

Key to level of contamination (outer bands) /RISK (inner bands)

High	Low	Safe	Pathogen Flow	Barrier

Figure 2   Generalised model illustrating the effect of different control measure in reducing health risks from wastewater reuse (WHO, 1989)

Figure 2, which show three combinations that can successfully protect the health of both workers and consumers. The feasibility and efficacy of any combination will depend on many factors, which must be considered carefully before any option is put into practice (Mara and Cairncross 1989). These factors will include the following:

a) Availability of resources (manpower, land, fund);

b) Existing social agricultural practice;

c) Existing patterns of excreta- related disease.

5.1 Pilot projects

First of all it will be worthwhile to study existing practices in the area, and possibly in the neighboring countries, before considering projects. Indeed, a government should at least consider how to ensure measures so that the current practices are not hazardous to health before embarking on a new development in the sector (Mara and Cairncross 1989). In Iran, as mentioned before, there is a problem of shortage of water; hence it is necessary to use polluted water as a source of irrigation of crops, which is already used without any serious control. In this way, the introduction of new techniques (for example, localized irrigation) is envisaged. The problem of health protection is only one of a number of intercommented questions that are difficult to answer without local experience of the kind that a pilot can give. These questions are likely to include important technical and economic aspects, including the feasibility of the scheme itself. Therefore the preliminary trials, on a pilot scale will often be essential anyway (Mara and Cairncross 1989).

A number of experiments for pilot plants in Tehran have been carried out by TRWA in designing domestic sewage treatment plant in Tehran. However it was considered before the finalization of sewage network, the treatment plant will treat part of surface waters which is running in current research area and west part of the city for irrigation.

Tables 32 to 34 shows the results of pilot plants which were studied for five and half months about surface water in the South of Tehran which comes from the west area of the city, two months mixing of water in the area under current research and west of Tehran and two months of the water in this study. Pilot plant consisted of primary treatment, which was sedimentation tank, and secondary treatment contained conventional activated sludge and secondary sedimentation.

Determinand	Percentage of removal in primary treatment	Percentage of total removal in primary and secondary treatment
BOD_5	50	93
COD	51	92
TSS	71	95
T. Nitrogen	34	44
Phosphate	29	44
Oil and Grease	50	87
Detergent	34	88
Fe	66	87
Cr	54	76
Zn	51	65
Al	59	83
Cu	63	84
Pb	41	57
Co	22	40
Ni	35	48
Cd	20	33

Table 32 Five and a half months pilot plant result for surface water in west of Tehran (From August 1999to January 2000)

A covered canal called Firooz Abad canal collects surface water in the west of Tehran. A pilot project for this canal was carried out from 9th of August 1999 to January 2000, which is illustrated in Table 32 as mentioned previously.

Determinand	Percentage of removal in primary treatment	Percentage of total removal in primary and secondary treatment
BOD$_5$	45	97
COD	46	94
TSS	59	97
T. Nitrogen	26	34
Phosphate	25	42
Oil and Grease	66	91
Detergent	31	74
Fe	49	92
Cr	58	90
Zn	57	77
Al	56	94
Cu	58	88
Pb	45	80
Co	45	61
Ni	35	48
Cd	31	44

Table 33 Two Months of pilot plant results for mixing surface water in the west and current research area in Tehran (From late January to late March 2000)

Determinand	Percentage of removal in primary treatment	Percentage of total removal in primary and secondary treatment
BOD$_5$	43	91
COD	44	78
TSS	65	92
T. Nitrogen	25	31
Phosphate	26	37
Oil and Grease	60	86
Detergent	21	87
Fe	66	92
Cr	51	90
Zn	64	86
Al	73	98
Cu	66	89
Pb	63	95
Co	82	95
Ni	49	63
Cd	89	96

Table 34 Two months of pilot plant results for surface water in current research area in Tehran (From late March to late May 2000)

The results of pilot projects could be useful as a guide for designing treatment plant in the area under research, however it has some deficits in the design of treatment plant for irrigation which are as follows.

1)   Length of experiment was two months while at least a period of one year studying is necessary

2)   Some determinands which are important in crop cultivation and potential hazard to public health do not exist in the pilot projects, for example TDS, Cl, Na, K, Ca, H CO3, NO3, NO2, number of helminth eggs, Borne, Total faecal coliform, and free chlorine

6.   Conclusions

a) The standard of water for irrigation in Iran at the present time is not suitable for a variety of climatic conditions, as well as the type of crops, which are cultivated in Iran. It has some deficiencies and the amount of some determinands has not been taken as reasonable.

b) It takes a long time to bring the water, in the network of stream, to the desired quality. Before this is done, the necessity of research on the treatment of this water for agricultural use is of great importance.

c) Comparison of the measured determinands with the standard values indicates the biological unsuitability of water for agricultural purposes. The potential health hazards are:

i) Germ problem due to the high quantity of coliforms contents.

ii) Helminth problem being 10 to 12 times above the standard level.

d) Considering the high number of total coliforms in station 7, it is suggested that examinations of this water for measuring the bacteria and viruses should be carried out.

e) The use of this water in agricultural purposes has a minor chemical problem.

By taking into account that Tehran is a part of Iran which has an arid and semi arid climatic condition, the shortage of water is a major problem. Hence it is necessary to use this water which amounts to around 156 (10^6 * cubic meters per year, efficiently. However due to the existence of biological problems such as helminth eggs and germs, it is suggested that:

1) At the first stage, suitable strategy is the combination of crop restriction and primary treatment. This method needs strong regulation and effective administration to enforce, which can be administered with the contribution of the Agriculture Ministry, TRWA, and DOE in Iran. If government requires some amendation in existing legislation or new laws, they can be suggested to the parliament.

2) For the prevention of possible contacts with people living around this network of streams with the contaminated water, it is necessary that adequate advice and warning be provided.

3) For the implementation of the third strategy, it is vital to carry out pilot plants at least four seasons, which farmers cultivate crops, as they need water for irrigation. However one year experiment for the appropriate design of the treatment plant is recommended. At this stage of treatment the removal of helminth eggs, faecal coliform and some chemical compounds at standard level which cause hazard for both human being and plants can be carried out.

f) Farmers and workers in this area should be trained in order to obey and follow the standard of hygiene regarding agricultural workers. These trainings may include:

Note:

* The amount of water is computed from forecast data Asadollahfardi,2002)

    i) Washing and rinsing those parts of the body and equipment which are contaminated.

    ii) The use of protecting materials and covers for farmers and workers.

Refrences

Aikman, D. I. (1983). Wastewater Reuse from Standpoint of Irrigated Agriculture, Journal of the Institution of Public Health Engineers, Vol. 11, No. 1, January, pp. 35-41.

Ali, I. (1987). Wastewater Criteria for Irrigation in Arid Regions, Journal of Irrigation and Drainage Engineering, ASCE Vol. 113, No. 2, , pp. 173-183.

AWWA (1985). Proceedings of Water Reuse Symposium *III*, Research Foundation, Denver, COLO, USA.

Asano, T. and Pettygrove, S. (1985). Irrigation with Reclaimed Municipal wastewater *Water for* agricultural using Reclaimed wastewater, Lewis Publishers

Asadollahfardi,G.(2002) ,Analysis of surface water quality in Tehran,Water quality research journal of Canda,37(2),489-511.

Alfarra,A. Kemp-Benedict,E. ,Hotzl,H.Sader,N. and Sonneveld,B.(2011) A framework   for wastewater reuse in Jordan utilizing a modified wastewater reuse index, Water Resource Mangement, 25,1153-1167.

Alfarra, A. Kemp-Benedict, E. Hötzl, H. ·Sader, N. and Sonneveld, B.(2011) A Framework for Wastewater Reuse in Jordan: utilizing a modified wastewater Reuse Index, Water Resource Management , 25,1153–1167.

Al Salem, S.S. and Abouzaid, H.(2006) Wastewater reuse for agriculture:regional health perspective, Eastern Mediterranean Health Journal, 12(3/4), 446-458.

Ayres, R. S. and Tanji, K. K. (1981). Agronomic Aspects of Crop Irrigation with Wastewater, Proceeding Water Forum, ASCE, Vol. 81, No. 1, pp. 579- 586, New York, USA.

Bouwer H. and Idelovitch, E. (1987). Quality Requirements for Irrigation with Sewage Water, Journal of Irrigation and Drainage Engineering, ASCE, Vol. 113, No. 4, November, pp. 516-535.

Blumenthal,U.J.Duncan.Mara ,D.Peasey, A.Ruiz-Palacios,G.and Stott,R.(2000) Guidelines for microbiological quality of treated wastewater used in agriculture:recommendations for revising WHO guideline,WHO,Bulltin ,78(9).

BlumenthalU. J. Enrique Cifuentes 't,E. Bennett, S. Quigley, M. and Ruiz-Palacios, G.(2001) The risk of enteric infections associated with wastewater reuse: the effect of season and degree of storage of wastewater, Transactions of Royal society of tropical medicine and hygiene,95,131-137.

Burfield, I. (1977). "Public Health Aspects of Nitrates in Essex Water Supplies, The Public Health Engineer, Vol. 5, No. 5, pp. 116-124, September.

Baier, D. C. and Fryer, W. B. (1973). Undesirable Plant Responses with Sewage Irrigation, Journal of the irrigation and drainage division, Vol. 99, No. (IR2), June, PP. 144-141.

Bixio,D. Thoeye,C. De Koning,J .Joksimovic ,D .Savic,D.Wintgens,T.nd Melin, T.(2006) Wastewater reuse in Europe Desalination,187,89-101.

Carr, G. Nortcliff, S. and Potter, R. B. (2010) Water reuse for irrigated agriculture in Jordan: challenges of soil sustainability and the role of management strategies, Phil. Trans. R. Soc. A , 368, 5315–5321.

Capra, A. Scicolone, B. (2004) Emitter and filter tests for wastewater reuse by drip irrigation, Agricultural water management, 68 (2), 135-149.

Cowan, J. P. and Johnson, P. R. (1984). Reuse of Effluent for Agriculture in the Middle East, Reuse of Sewage Effluent. Proceeding of the International Symposium Organised by the Institution of Civil Engineers held in London on 30-31 October

Crawford, R. F. and Kennedy, W. K. (1960). Nitrates in Forage Crops and Silage: Benefice Hazards, Precautions, Cornell Miscellaneous Bulletin, No. 37, June, pp. 5-14.

Crook, J. (1978). Health Aspects of Water Reuse in California, Journal of the Environmental Engineering Division, ASCE, Vol. 104, pp. 601-610.

Environmental Protection Institute (DOE)(1994). Standard for Sewage Discharge, Technical Report, Tehran, Iran (In Persian language).

El Ayni, F. Cherif, S Jrad A. Trabelsi-Ayadi, M. (2011) Impact of Treated Wastewater Reuse on Agriculture and Aquifer Recharge in a Coastal Area: Korba Case Study Water Resource Management , 25,2251–2265.

Fatwa (religious ruling), on the Use of Recycled Wastewater for Religious Purposes, (1979). Al-Madinah Newspaper, Jeddah, Saudi Arabia, Apr. 17, pp. 2.

Feachem, R. G. and Blum, D. (1984). Health Aspects of Wastewater Reuse of Sewage Effluent. Proceeding of the International Symposium Organised by the Institution of Civil Engineers held in London on 30-31 October 1984.

Hart, B. T. (1974).Compilation of Australian Water Resources Council Technical Paper, No. 7 Research Project No. 71/36, Caulfied Institute of Technology, Canberra, Australian Government Publishing Services.

Israeli Ministry of Health (1979). Recommendations for Treatment of Wastewater to be used for Crop Irrigation, 2nd Draft, Israeli Ministry of Health, Nov.

Israeli Ministry of Health (1981). Purification of Sewage Water to be used for Irrigation, Public Health Law, No. 4263, Israeli Ministry of Health Aug., 27.

Jenkins, W. O. (1988). Decision Support System in River Basin Management, PhD Thesis, Imperial College, University of London.

Jimenez B. (2005) Treatment technology and standard for agricultural wastewater reuse: a case study in Mexico, Irrigation and Drainage, 54, S23–S33.

Katzenelson, E.; Buium, I. and Shuval, H. I. (1976). Risk of Communicable Disease Infection Associated with Wastewater Irrigation in Agricultural Settlements, Science, Vol. 194, pp. 944-946.

Lopeza, A. Pollicea, A. Lonigrob, A. Masic, S. Palesed, A.M. Cirellie, G.L.,

Toscanoe, A. Passinoa, R. (2006) Agricultural wastewater reuse in southern Italy, Desalination 187 ,323–334

Mara, D. and Cairncross, S. (1989). Guidelines for the Safe Use of Wastewater and Excreta in Agriculture and Aquaculture, Geneva, World Health Organisation

Police, A. Lopez, A. Laera, G. Rubino, P. and Lonigro, A. (2004) Tertiary filtered municipal wastewater as an alternative water resource source in agriculture: a field investigation in Southern Italy, Science of the Total Environment, 324, 201–210.

Rains, D. W. (1971). Lead Accumulation by Wild Oats (Avena Latua) in a Contaminated Area, Nature, Vol. 233, No. 5316, September 17, pp. 210-211.

Ranieri, E. Harold Leverenz, H. and Tchobanoglous, G. (2011) An Examination of the factors involved in Agricultural Reuse: Technologies, Regulatory and Social Aspects, Journal of Water Resource and Protection, 3, 300-310.

Shuval,H.Lampert,Y. and Fattal,B.(1997) Development of a risk assessment approach for evaluating wastewater reuse standard for agriculture, Water Science Technology, 35 (11-12), 15-20.

Srikanth, R. and Naik, D. (2004) Prevalence of Giardiasis due to wastewater reuse for agriculture in the suburbs of Asmara City, Eritrea , International Journal of

Environmental Health Research, 14 (1), 43 – 52.

Uriu, K. (1971). The Influence of Cultural Problems on the Quality of 'Dixon' Cling Peaches, Research Progress Report, University of California, Davis Pomology, April, p. 12.

US Environmental Protection Agency, (1992). Guideline for Wastewater Reused, Cincinnati, EPA Publisher.

WHO, (1973). Reuse of Effluents: Methods of Wastewater Treatment and Health Safeguards, *Report of WHO Meeting of Experts*, Technical Report Series No. 517, held at Geneva, Switzerland.

Yang, H. Abbaspour., K. C., (2007) Analysis of wastewater reuse potential in Beijing, Desalination , 212, 238–250.

Appendix A

A. TABLE OF SOME OF THE COMMUNICABLE DISEASES

In this appendix, some informations on the communicable diseases related to the use of polluted water together with their methods of transmission and prevention are given in a tabulated form below:-

Disease	Description	Transmission	Preventation
Ascaris	Helminthic infection of small intestine	By ingestion of infective helminthic eggs from soil contaminated from human faece	Encourage satisfactory hygiene provisions for fecal disposal
Champh y-lobacter	Acute enteric disease	Ingestion of organisms in contaminated food or waste	Adequate cooking of food Hygiene esp . with animals
Hookwo rm	Chronic diseased cause by intestinal infection by nematodes	Deposition of eggs in faeces with subsequent penetration of hatched larvae through skin	Sanitary facilities Health Education
Hepatiti s A	Viral infection	Person to person by the faecal-oral route	Education towards good sanitation and hygiene
Guineaw o-rm	Tissue infection by nematode	Larvae deposited from worm escape from the infected part of body on immersion in water	Provision of potable water Restrict human/water contact
Giardias is	Protozoan infection	Contaminated water supplies or from faecally contaminated food	Disposal of faeces . Protect potable water supplies
Seabies	Contamination of mites	Skin contact or from contaminated linen ect .	Health Education
Shigella	Bacterial disease	Faecal-oral transmission	Promote hygienic practices
Trachom a	Vascular invasion of cornea with progressive visual disability	Contact with discharge from mucus etc .of infected person	Education in hygiene

Table A.1   Some of the communicable diseases (Jenkins , 1988)

cont/d...

59

Disease	Description	Transmission	Preventation
Strongylo-idiasis	Helminthic infection	Penetration of skin by larvae after faecal deposition of eggs	Sanitary disposal of excreta Improve hygiene
Rotavirus	Viral gastric infection	Faecal oral or faecal respiratory route	Hygiene
Dengue	Viral infection	Bites of infected mosquito	Eliminate vector mosquito breeding places (still water)
Typhoid	Bacterial infection	Contact with faeces or urine of carrier , esp in food and water	Sanitary disposal of faeces proect water supplies Hygienic food preparation
Cholera	Acute intestinal disease	Primarily ingestion of faecally contaminated	As above
Schistoso-miasis	Trematod infection	Introduction of eggs into water from urine or faeces of carrier development of larvae in intermediate snail host . larvae penetrate human skin	Faecal disposal facilities Reduce snail habitats Restrict man/water contact
Typhus	Bacterial	Transmitted by lice and fleas	
Malaria	Protozoan infection	Transmitled by mosquito	Elimination of vectors Improve living conditions
Polio	Viral disease	Direct contact , faecal-oral or pharyngeal spread	Immunise , Health Education
Yellow fever	Viral infection	Mosquito	Endicate mosquito vector Reduce breeding grounds
W. Bancrofti	Mosquito	Mosquito	Endicate mosquito vector Reduce breeding grounds (still contaminated water)
On chocarcias-is	Parasitic nematode	Bite of infected flies	Endicate mosquito vector Reduce breeding grounds (fast running streams)

Continued   *Table A.1*

this paperback is printed by

reha gmbh
Dudweilerstraße 72
66111 Saarbrücken
www.rehagmbh.de